The Victorian Clergyman

Trevor May

Christopher Wordsworth (1807–85) personifies many aspects of the Victorian clergyman. He was the son of the Reverend Christopher Wordsworth, Master of Trinity College, Cambridge, and a nephew of the poet. After a distinguished career at Cambridge, he was ordained in 1835 but, like many of a scholarly bent, he did not immediately take up parochial work. Instead, in 1836 he became Headmaster of Harrow School. He was not a success there, and in 1844 the Prime Minister, Sir Robert Peel (himself an Old Harrovian), appointed him a Canon of Westminster. In the Church he was more successful. In 1850 Wordsworth accepted the living of Stanford in the Vale, now in Oxfordshire, serving for nearly twenty years as a parish priest. In 1869 he became Bishop of Lincoln, where he expended over £6000 of his own money in establishing a training college for ordinands. He also revived the use of the cope, a matter of some controversy. Wordsworth was a prolific writer, both of scholarly books and of hymns, publishing well over one hundred of the latter, a few of which still remain popular. He represents a dynastic element in the Church, for his brother, Charles, was Bishop of St Andrews, while his son, John (died 1911), was Bishop of Salisbury.

Contents

The Victorian Church 3

Becoming a clergyman 11

Incumbents and curates 15

The professionalisation of the clergy 21

Worship, preaching and liturgy 28

Town church and cathedral close 34

Further reading 39

Places to visit 40

Cover: *Detail from 'Signing the Marriage Register' (1896), a painting by James Charles (1851–1906). (© Bradford Art Galleries and Museums, West Yorkshire, UK/The Bridgeman Art Library)*

ACKNOWLEDGEMENTS
Illustrations are acknowledged as follows: Dorset County Museum, pages 4, 23 (bottom); London Borough of Harrow Local History Library, page 5; by permission of the Warden and Fellows of Keble College, Oxford, page 7 (top); the Kilvert Society, page 16 (top).

British Library Cataloguing in Publication Data: May, Trevor. The Victorian Clergyman. – (Shire album; 459) 1. Church of England – Clergy – History – 19th century 2. Church of England – History – 19th century 3. Clergy – England – History – 19th century 4. England – Religion – 19th century I. Title 283.4'2'09034. ISBN-10: 0 7478 0658 6. ISBN-13: 978 0 7478 0658 5.

Published by Shire Publications Ltd, Midland House, West Way, Botley, Oxford OX2 0PH, UK.
(Website: www.shirebooks.co.uk)
Copyright © 2006 by Trevor May. First published 2006. Transferred to digital print on demand 2011.
Shire Album 459. ISBN 978 0 74780 658 5. Trevor May is hereby identified as the author of this work in accordance with Section 77 of the Copyright, Designs and Patents Act 1988.

Printed by PrintOnDemandWorldwide.com, Peterborough, UK.

The Victorian Church

This book is about Victorian clergymen of the Church of England, but in order to understand who they were, what they believed and what they did it is first necessary to say something about the Victorian Church itself. Since the Reformation the Anglican Church had been something of a 'bridge church' between Roman Catholicism on the one hand and more extreme Protestantism on the other. Such being the case, it was inevitable that tensions would be felt within it, as they are to this day. The Church of England in the nineteenth century was no monolith and incorporated distinct wings, with 'Low Church' Evangelicals on the one hand and 'High Church' Tractarians on the other. At the same time there were followers of a more liberal 'Broad Church', as well as adherents to 'Christian Socialism'. The party to which a clergyman was sympathetic coloured his theology, the way he worshipped, the manner in which he set out and furnished his church, and even the way he dressed.

Secondly, while historians find it convenient to carve up the past into periods such as the 'Victorian Age', it would be equally unreasonable to suppose that during the period of Queen Victoria's reign there were no changes or trends as it would be to assert that the accession or death of the monarch provided a sharp division with the periods which preceded or succeeded it. Indeed, in the fifty years before the Queen's accession many so-called 'Victorian values' came to prominence, not least in the field of religion. In 1787 George III issued a Proclamation against Vice and Immorality, condemning blasphemy, Sabbath-breaking and drunkenness. The eighteenth century had been one of great brutality, both public and private, with two hundred offences punishable by death. It was also a century in which the very nature and

In 'The Sleeping Congregation' (1736) the painter and engraver William Hogarth satirised the somnolent state of the Church of England. The clergyman is reading Matthew, chapter 11, verse 28: 'Come unto me, all ye that labour and are heavy laden, and I will give you rest.' The implication is that his own ecclesiastical burdens are not that heavy. Meanwhile, the clerk (seated in the lower tier of the double-decker pulpit) glances sideways at the exposed bosoms of the young woman, whose reading suggests that she is dreaming of marriage. At his installation as Archdeacon of York in 1751, Dr Edmund Pyle experienced a similar temptation as that which faced the clerk: 'Nothing but ladies by dozens (and very pretty ones) on the right hand or the left or in front of my stall, but through mercy, having the service to read I was forced to look at least as much on the rubric of the book as upon that of their cheeks.'

BLANDFORD.

SEIZURE

FOR

CHURCH RATES.

The Churchwardens of this Parish, Mr. W. T. Elgar and Mr. Robert Lock, in the exercise of the *Legal Authority* which they possess to *compel* those who dissent from the CHURCH OF ENGLAND, to contribute towards the support of its worship, have caused to be seized

TWO CARTS,

from Mr. H. F. FISHER, in payment of £4. 2. 10, the amount of RATE demanded.

The Carts were disposed of in the Market Place, by Mr. Clarke, of Wimborne — the Auctioneers of this Town refusing to co-operate in such an unpopular undertaking. The amount realized was £5. 2. 6, the real value of the property being about £10.

It is unnecessary to comment on the *unscriptural character of the above proceedings.*

April 27th. 1859.

BY THE CHURCH.

A PROCLAMATION,

WHEREAS certain Inhabitants of this Parish, on the plea of conscientious objections and other pretences, did refuse to comply with our demand for money, not only to repair the Church but to pay for washing the surplice, and the bread and wine for the Ordinance, &c. ;

AND WHEREAS our trusty and beloved Constable acting under a "Distress Warrant," in that case provided, did enter the Farm-yard of one of the persons aforesaid, and for Rates and the cost of recovering the same, did seize and take Two Carts of the Value of ten Pounds and upwards.

AND WHEREAS such articles being now our lawful property, we do will that the same be converted into the current coin of this Realm, and have authorised our respected Auctioneer by stroke of the hammer to sell and dispose of such articles to the highest bidder for the same.

AND WHEREAS sundry persons, not holding us in due reverence, and aiding and abetting the rescuants aforesaid, wickedly declare that we have been guilty of Robbery in making such seizure, and in divers ways incite opposition to the Sale thereof.

AND WHEREAS if such evil counsels prevail there will be few bidders at such Sale, and our faithful Churchwardens will be exposed to loss which only our enemies ought to suffer ;

AND WHEREAS our Church must fall without such CHRISTIAN means of support;

WE THEREFORE strictly enjoin and command all our Loyal and Loving Children to attend the Sale, that then and there, by their bidding they may uphold our lawful authority, and testify that these our Laws and Usages are in accordance with GOD'S HOLY WORD, and needful for our continued existance and welfare.

GOD SAVE THE CHURCH!

Church rates, raised for the upkeep of the church fabric, were levied on all parishioners, whether Anglicans or Dissenters. Churchwardens had the power to distrain goods for non-payment, though such an inflammatory procedure was generally avoided. These two posters, relating to the auction of seized goods, come from Blandford Forum, in Dorset. They testify to the acrimony that church rates could cause.

structure of society were ravaged by the forces of industrialisation. To all of this the Church needed to respond, which it slowly did.

The spiritual temperature of the Church was low in the eighteenth century, but there yet remained many faithful clergymen dedicated to a vital religion going beyond superficial religious observance or mere decent living. Many who felt such a 'call to seriousness' were drawn to John Wesley and to Methodism. Wesley, ordained an Anglican priest in 1728, tried to keep the new movement within the Church, but (as a Methodist writer put it in 1834) he was like an oarsman who faced the Church of England while he steadily rowed away from it. The spirit of Methodism did pervade large sections of the Church, however, and many clergy and lay people who were influenced by Wesley's ideas, but chose to remain within the Church, formed the backbone of the group that came to be known as the Evangelicals.

W. E. Gladstone estimated that by the late 1820s one-eighth of Anglican clergy were Evangelical, while at mid century the proportion had risen to between a third and a half. Yet at the height of the early nineteenth-century Evangelical revival most of the leading figures were lay people, a circumstance that is not surprising given the movement's emphasis on personal judgement and individual responsibility and endeavour. Evangelical Christians did not tamely leave moral

J. W. Cunningham (1780–1861) was a prominent Evangelical, having served as a curate with John Venn, one of the leaders of the Clapham Sect. In 1811 he became vicar of Harrow, where he remained until his death. Cunningham was the model for the Vicar of Wrexhill in the eponymous novel by Frances Trollope, whose son, Anthony, was a pupil at Harrow School. This satirical engraving, entitled 'The Cunning Man of Harrow', suggests that he was a windbag, which may have been true, though in a somewhat less devilish way than here depicted. The subject is drawn from Cunningham's observation that 'If I had a thousand hands and a thousand sledge hammers in them, I would use them all... in endeavouring to sweep from the face of the earth that detested and abominable monster, POPERY'. The antagonism shown by many Evangelicals towards Roman Catholics was matched by their loathing of those Anglicans they suspected of bringing Romanising tendencies into the Church of England.

THE CUNNING MAN of HARROW

judgements to the Church hierarchy.

Many of the early reformers congregated at Clapham in south London and worshipped in the parish church, of which John Venn was rector between 1792 and 1813. The 'Clapham Sect', as it came to be called, included Henry Thornton, a wealthy banker, whose _Family Prayers_, published in 1834, ran to over thirty editions within two years and made a great contribution to the domestic worship of a generation of middle-class families. Of greater influence was William Wilberforce, who had been principal instigator of the Proclamation against Vice and Immorality. The head of a large commercial house in Hull, Wilberforce was the power behind the anti-slavery movement, which secured the abolition of the slave trade in 1807. 'Well, Henry, what shall we abolish next?', Wilberforce is said to have asked Thornton after the final debate in the House of Commons. This enthusiasm for social action placed the Evangelicals at the forefront of reform movements, where they pioneered many of the techniques of pressure-group politics.

Life flowed back into the Church through the Evangelicals, but the individual responsibility which was their strength also had its down side. Their insistence on a conversion experience, an instantaneous turning from darkness to the light, ignored the experience of countless Christians whose spiritual journey was one of gradual illumination, and Evangelicals could succumb to bigotry and a holier-than-thou attitude.

Evangelicalism was a response to rapid economic and social change, but revival in the Church is never a once-and-for-all phenomenon. By the 1830s Evangelicalism appeared to be something of a spent force, and reinvigoration had to be looked for elsewhere. It was from the High Church end of the Anglican spectrum that the next reform movement came, and it was initially a response to political events.

The Church of England was the established church and, as such, had a special relationship with the State which was not enjoyed by other denominations. Bishops were appointed by the Crown on the advice of the Prime Minister, and as 'Lords Spiritual' they held seats in the upper chamber of Parliament, the House of Lords. Though only twenty-six in number, they sometimes exercised a strong influence on legislation. Nowhere was this more apparent than in the attempts to reform the franchise. In October 1831 the first Reform Bill was thrown out by the House of Lords, where only two bishops voted in favour. There were anti-Church demonstrations in many places, and at Bristol the Bishop's palace was burned down. Four of the perpetrators were subsequently hanged. The anti-Catholic sentiments of the ensuing Guy Fawkes Night were supplemented by resentment towards the Church of England. At Crayford in Kent the revellers sang:

> Remember, remember
> That God is the sender
> Of every good gift unto man;
> But the devil, to spite us,
> Sent fellows in mitres
> Who rob us of all that they can.

Many people objected to the Church's wealth and to the manner in which that wealth was distributed. In 1832 *The Times* published a short poem in which St Jerome returned to earth in order to make a tour of the Church of England. He visited Durham, where William van Mildert was Bishop. There,

> He found that pious soul van Mildert
> Much with his money-bags bewildered.

The finances of Durham were, indeed, bewildering. Each of the twelve canons received £3000 a year, while the Reverend Francis Egerton, eccentric eighth Earl of Bridgewater, held a financially rewarding prebend for forty-nine years, during which he lived in Paris. It was in order to put the cathedral endowments in order before they were confiscated that, in the same year, the chapter resolved to establish the University of Durham.

In 1835 the government established an Ecclesiastical Duties and Revenues Commission, reconstituted the following year as the Ecclesiastical Commission, a permanent body charged with reforming the structure of the Church. The Church had no machinery of its own to achieve this object, which could be brought about only by the passage through Parliament of enforceable legislation. This ascendancy of the State over the Church (known as Erastianism) aroused the ire of many in the Church of England. Their suspicions were raised by the experience of the Anglican Church in Ireland.

Since the Act of Union of 1801 the government at Westminster had become responsible for over seven million Irish people, of whom around five and a half million were Roman Catholic. Most Irish regarded the Anglican Church as heretical and intrusive, and there was a general refusal to pay tithes and church rates. In the interest of restoring order, in 1833 Parliament suppressed or amalgamated a number of Irish dioceses, the incomes of which were to be redistributed among the poorer clergy.

John Keble (1792–1866) was the son of a Gloucestershire vicar. He attended the University of Oxford, where in 1811 he became a fellow of Oriel College. There he encountered E. B. Pusey and John Henry Newman, with whom he founded the Oxford Movement. Seven of the 'Tracts for the Times' came from his pen. Keble was described as a shy, homely and unambitious man, who turned down several offers of preferment because of the poor health of his father. In 1827 he published 'The Christian Year', a collection of poems (many made into hymns) to be used as daily readings. The book was immensely popular and ran to over a hundred editions by the year that he died. He ploughed the profits into the restoration of Hursley church in Hampshire, where he had become vicar in 1836. He was an exemplary parish priest, many of his parishioners not realising that he was a national figure within the Church of England. In 1869 Keble College, Oxford, was founded as a memorial.

The parliamentary reform of the Church in Ireland aroused a deep suspicion among anti-Erastians in the Church of England, who feared that events would lead to the disestablishment of the Church, and to a loss of its privileges. They emphasised the apostolic heritage of the Church, its mandate received from Christ, the Head of the Church, and transmitted by His apostles to their successors, the bishops. It was the ascended Christ, not the State, who commissioned the Church and set out its task. This was the thrust of the ground-breaking assize sermon which John Keble preached at Oxford in 1833 and which many saw as the birth of the Oxford Movement.

This new movement was led by John Henry Newman, John Keble and Edward Pusey, all fellows of Oriel College. Against the somewhat narrow and individualistic thinking of Evangelicalism, they stressed continuity within the Church of England, which remained part of one catholic and apostolic Church. They stressed the importance of ceremonies handed down from the past, and they developed a keen interest in liturgy and ritual, and in architecture and church vestments. To an age steeped in the romanticism and medievalism of Sir Walter Scott, this struck a powerful chord. The ideas of the Oxford reformers were propagated through a

The restoration of the Roman Catholic hierarchy into England in 1850 provoked a strong reaction, which inevitably rubbed off on the Oxford Movement. Here, the 'Punch' cartoonist depicts an undergraduate going to lectures with a papal crown tucked under his mortar board.

Thomas Arnold (1795–1842) is best known as the headmaster of Rugby School, from where he set in motion the reform of public schools throughout England; but he was also an important figure in the Church. He was an undergraduate with John Keble at Corpus Christi College, Oxford, and like him he went on to be a fellow of Oriel College. Arnold had a loathing of Tractarianism, however. He observed: 'I look upon a Roman Catholic as an enemy in his uniform; I look upon a Tractarian as an enemy disguised as a spy.' He was no more sympathetic to the Low Church, defining an Evangelical as 'a good Christian, with a low understanding, a bad education, and ignorance of the world'. Arnold's liberal and at times unorthodox views kept him from preferment, but he was acknowledged as an important influence on those who favoured a Broad Church.

series of *Tracts for the Times*, from which derived their alternative title of Tractarians. They were works of considerable scholarship, aimed at the clergy rather than the laity, and their emphasis on the priestly role provided a new basis for the increased professionalism that was creeping into the Church. Altogether, some ninety *Tracts* were issued between 1833 and 1842, the series coming to an abrupt end with the furore over publication of *Tract XC*, in which Newman argued that the Thirty-nine Articles, the defining formulary of Anglican doctrine, were not substantially different from the theology of the Roman Catholic Church. As in the past, when those of an Evangelical persuasion had to choose between Methodism and remaining in the Anglican fold, so now High Churchmen found a door open to Rome. Between 1840 and 1899, some 446 Tractarian clergy were received into the Roman Catholic Church, including Newman himself, in 1845.

Charles Kingsley (1818–75) served a curacy at Eversley in Hampshire and was offered the living in 1844. He was a great campaigner for the poor, whose cause he pleaded through both pamphlets and novels. 'Alton Locke' (1850) looked at the plight of urban workers, while 'Yeast' (1851) examined the lives of the rural poor. His children's book 'The Water Babies', which considered the treatment of young chimney sweeps, first appeared in 1863. Kingsley was a prominent member of the Christian Socialists, a rather loose group that engaged in social work and adult education, the guiding ideal being the application of Christian principles to all social relationships. Echoing Karl Marx, he wrote that the Bible had been reduced to a 'mere special constable's handbook, an opium dose for keeping beasts of burden patient while they were being overloaded'. Although his health was poor, he had a great love of the outdoors and was a leading exponent of 'Muscular Christianity', a label that he loathed.

Left: *The plethora of groups within the Church of England complicated the task of finding a curate congenial to the incumbent. 'Hedging' is the title of this 'Punch' cartoon of 1879, to which the caption runs:*
  Rector. 'And what are your views?'
  Candidate for Curacy. 'Well, Sir, I'm an Evangelical High Churchman, of liberal opinions.'

Below left: *Archbishop Edward White Benson (1829–96) on his horse, Columba. Benson had never been a parish priest but for thirteen years was headmaster of Wellington College. He became first Bishop of Truro in 1877, and Archbishop of Canterbury five years later. It was said of him that 'horses and riding were his unfailing delight'. For him, riding was a matter of pleasure rather than necessity. For the country clergyman, however, possession of a horse greatly facilitated travel around an often extensive parish that would otherwise have to be covered on foot. The Reverend Octavius Pickard-Cambridge, for example, estimated that he had walked seven thousand miles between his church at Bloxworth, in Dorset, and the neighbouring church at Winterborne Tomson, for which he was also responsible.*

Right: *This statue of Bishop Reginald Heber (1783–1826) is to be found in Calcutta Cathedral, from which he maintained oversight of a diocese which, in his day, covered the whole of India. He is perhaps best known for his hymns, which include 'Brightest and best of the sons of the morning' and the now less frequently sung 'From Greenland's icy mountains'.*

Left: *This commemorative plate marking Queen Victoria's Golden Jubilee in 1887 noted, in its central roundel, that she ruled an 'Empire on which the sun never sets'. But by then the Church of England was part of an Anglican Communion even more extensive than the British Empire, for it included the Episcopal Church of the United States. In 1888 a total of 211 bishops were invited to the Lambeth Conference.*

FASHIONS FOR 1850; OR,   **A PAGE FOR THE PUSEYITES.**

Any exaggerated form of dress, secular, military or clerical, was sure to be lampooned in 'Punch', which always seemed to be able to find some innovation to ridicule. Early in 1851 it was bloomers, arising from the visit to England of the American social reformer Mrs Amelia Bloomer. In the previous year it had been the turn of the Puseyites, whose fads, 'Punch' surmised, if unchecked, would soon spread to women and children and even to footmen.

Those Tractarians who remained in the Church of England faced many obstacles, but they left a rich legacy. Of greatest significance was the encouragement they gave to the clergy to acknowledge and develop their priestly role, to engage in deeper scholarship and to pay more vigorous attention to pastoral care. By the end of the century many of their ideas, anathematised by some at first, had permeated the whole Church.

It is easy to see Evangelicalism and Tractarianism as polar, an assumption apparently justified by the heat of nineteenth-century religious controversies, but, as in party politics, it was tempting for opponents to exaggerate their differences. The historian Horton Davies puts it like this:

> Each side seemed, if not to deny, at least to undervalue, what had hitherto been part of its heritage and the result was lop-sidedness. If the High Churchman stressed the importance of the sacramental life, then the fear of approximation to Roman Catholicism caused the Evangelicals to exalt preaching the more, to make less of the Sacraments, and to refuse to make any change in their Prayer Book worship. Similarly, the Tractarians who had spread their distinctive tenets more effectively from the pulpit of St Mary-the-Virgin, Oxford, the University Church, than in their increasingly lengthy, erudite, and tendentious *Tracts for the Times*, were inclined in time to depreciate the subjectivity of preaching because the Evangelicals had made much more of it.

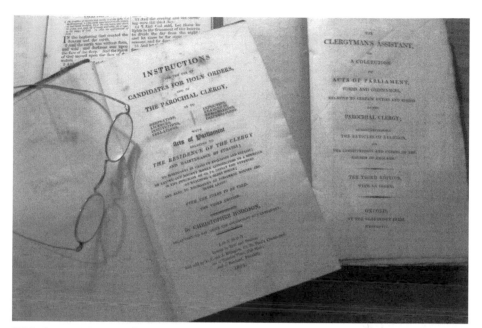

With clergy training virtually non-existent in the early nineteenth century, there was a large market for handbooks aiming to guide clergymen through the legal requirements of their office. The Bodleian Library at Oxford possesses around one hundred published between 1750 and 1875. Two examples, shown here, are 'The Clergyman's Assistant' of 1808 and 'Instructions for the Use of Candidates for Holy Orders and of the Parochial Clergy', published in 1824. The latter provided examples of the documentation required when a man presented himself for ordination.

Becoming a clergyman

In 1831 there were 10,718 Anglican clergy, rising to 17,821 twenty years later. In 1900 there were about 23,000 clergy in the Church of England. By 2006 the numbers had fallen dramatically: there were now around 9000 clergy (including women) involved in parochial work, as well as some 2000 unpaid.

The present-day idea that the priesthood is a vocation, a calling from God, has not always been the dominant factor when 'going into the Church'. In early times the Church was seen by many as the gateway into more remunerative occupations, especially when Church and State were so intertwined. The Church had a monopoly of learning in the Middle Ages, such that the word 'clerk' came to mean not only a cleric but also one who earned his living with the pen. To be able to read and write was presumed to indicate clerical status. Indeed, 'benefit of clergy', whereby clergy were exempt from trial in the secular courts, was later allowed on a first indictment for many offences to all who could read, a privilege abolished only in 1827.

By the end of the eighteenth century the Anglican priesthood was seen by many as a fitting occupation for a gentleman. It was untainted by vulgar money-making and offered a life of service, as did a commission in the Army. Better still, the service required of the clergyman need not be too onerous, leaving ample time for other gentlemanly pursuits, whether scholarly or sporting. There were other similarities

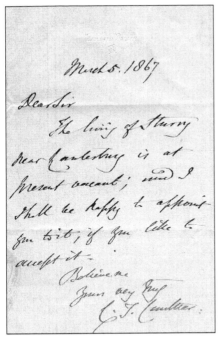

with the Army. Patronage was important to success in both careers and, although the purchase of commissions was abolished in 1871 (the same year that patronage in the civil service came to an end), patronage in the Church of England continues to this day, for clergy are still 'presented' to a living by a patron. That right of presentation to the Bishop, for him to install, is known as an advowson and was considered valuable property that could be sold or auctioned on the open market. Not until 1931 were parishioners, through the parochial church council, allowed a measure of choice over a new incumbent.

It was important, then, to have a patron. Diane McClatchey quotes James Palmer, curate of Headington, Oxfordshire, writing to a Balliol College friend in 1806:

> If I had been the nineteenth cousin of a Lord, I might have attained hopes of a living, but I have not one drop of Duke's blood in me that I know of, and have no one to patronize or assist me, so that probably I shall continue a curate all my life.

Sadly, this was truer than he realised, for two years later he was thrown from his horse and killed.

Nepotism was rife. Henry Fardell (1795–1854) was presented to Wisbech by his father-in-law, Bowyer Sparke, Bishop of Ely. So many of this prelate's relatives held ecclesiastical office in his diocese that it was said that one could find one's way through the Fens by the light of the Sparkes in the stubble.

The entry requirements for ordination were few, and not arduous. A man first had to be ordained deacon, the lower age limit for which was twenty-three, and he had to satisfy the Bishop as to his status, moral character and intellectual abilities. If ordained deacon, he generally proceeded to priest's orders, which could not be taken before the age of twenty-four. Before the 1840s ordinands simply had to demonstrate that they were 'learned in the Latin tongue and sufficiently instructed in the Scriptures'. Examination in the early part of the century was lax. The examining chaplain (and son-in-law) of Bishop North of Winchester examined two candidates in a tent on a cricket field, at moments when he was not engaged in the game. There is ample evidence that other examinations were equally cursory.

Some, like William Cooke Taylor in his book *The Bishop* (1841), argued that:

> A mere examination cannot give a prelate sufficient knowledge of the qualifications of a candidate; you are choosing a working clergyman, not a professor of dogmatic theology.

Even a graduate with a good degree might lack the necessary skills. He continued:

> If a clergyman knows not how to lead his flock in the right way, it is no compensation for those who go astray that he knows more Hebrew than a Jewish rabbi, or can solve mathematical problems which would have perplexed Newton.

While a degree from Oxford or Cambridge was virtually a *sine qua non*, these universities provided nothing like a professional education for clergy, in a practical or technical sense. In the early 1830s the Norrisian Professor of Divinity at Cambridge gave a testimonial to every student who had attended a course of twenty-five lectures, but there was no examination, and many students lounged around, reading a newspaper or a novel. Lectures were provided at Oxford leading to a testamur, but few opted to follow them. Neither university offered a degree course in theology until the 1870s.

The idea of theological colleges was slow to develop, and the earliest ones served

An old labourer is appalled to see that the parson is a Bachelor of Divinity. As he exclaims, 'Bachelor of Divinity! Then that there man ain't a right man to praich... 'cause he calls hisself a bachelor! An' I knows he's a married man.' In 1827–8, 91 per cent of ordinands were graduates of Oxford and Cambridge universities. By the last decades of the nineteenth century, 50 per cent still came from the same source, while a further 25 per cent were graduates of another university (mainly Durham). By the mid 1970s 42 per cent of ordinands did not have a university degree. The Bachelor of Divinity degree was a postgraduate degree, not held by most ordinands.

Charles John Vaughan (1816–97) was the son of a clergyman and went to Rugby School, where he came under the influence of Thomas Arnold. He was ordained in 1841 and, after a brief spell as vicar of St Martin's, Leicester, was appointed headmaster of Harrow School in 1844, where his teaching and preaching revived a languishing institution. He left after fifteen years and might have expected high preferment in the church, but personal reasons prevented this. In 1860 he became vicar of Doncaster. Here he entered upon remarkable work preparing young men for ordination, over one hundred passing through his hands before he accepted the mastership of the Temple (one of the London Inns of Court) in 1869. In 1879 he became Dean of Llandaff, where he continued his work with ordinands.

remote areas where it was difficult to find competent candidates for ordination. In the eighteenth century Bishop Thomas Wilson had established a college on the Isle of Man; and St Bee's College was formed in 1816 to serve Cumberland in a similar way. St David's College, Lampeter, was opened in 1831 to provide an approximation to an Oxford or Cambridge college and received its royal charter in 1833, a year after a small college at Durham was raised to university status. Bishop Otter College, Chichester, was founded in 1839, and in subsequent decades similar theological colleges were founded in a number of cathedral cities.

The theological colleges were not without their critics. As individual colleges became associated with particular parties in the Church, party spirit was strengthened. There was little uniformity in training, and scant central direction. And, of greatest importance to some critics, the colleges represented an invasion of professional training into a field still largely dominated by gentlemanly amateurishness. Anthony Trollope was not alone in thinking that gentlemen would be squeezed out by mere 'literates'. So, the going was slow, and it was not until 1909 that a period of residential training became mandatory for all ordinands.

Incumbents and curates

From earliest times the Church appreciated that provision had to be made for the maintenance of the clergy, and the Church of England dealt with this by Canon 33 of the Canons of 1604, which were part of ecclesiastical law:

> It hath been long since provided by many decrees of the ancient Fathers, that none should be admitted either Deacon or Priest, who had not first some certain place, where he might use his function. According to which examples we do ordain, that henceforth no person shall be admitted into Sacred Orders, except he shall at that time exhibit to the Bishop, of whom he desireth imposition of hands, a Presentation of himself to some Ecclesiastical Preferment then void in that diocese.

In other words, he had to have a job to go to, and that might include other kinds of preferment, such as a Fellowship at Oxford or Cambridge, for which ordination was a requirement till at least the 1870s. For deacon's orders, the candidate for ordination had to certify that he had a nomination to a curacy, and, for priest's orders, either nomination to a curacy or presentation to a living. The 'living' was the entitlement of the incumbent to the funds (mainly income from tithe or the glebe

A cartoon from 'Punch' in 1852 depicts a 'Genteel Pluralist' musing: 'What the people can want with a Crystal Palace on Sundays, I can't think! Surely they ought to be contented with their church, and their home afterwards.' Pluralism had been greatly reduced by the Pluralities Act of 1837, as amended in 1850; but the point here seems to be that the cathedral close (for this is no ordinary clergyman) was remote from the country cottage.

land) devoted to the clergy. Depending on the apportionment of the tithe he would have the title either of vicar or rector, but his duties were the same.

Livings varied enormously in value and, being based on agricultural values, were subject to fluctuation. The average income of incumbents was about £500 in 1837 but had fallen to £246 in 1897, although curates by that time were better paid than before. Averages, of course, hide a wide range. The richest living was Doddington in Cambridgeshire, which was worth £7300 until 1868. Stanhope in County Durham, at £4000 a year, was the second or third largest, receiving notoriety in 1830 when the incumbent, Henry Philpotts, was appointed Bishop of Exeter and proposed to retain his living in order to supplement his meagre episcopal stipend of £3500 a year. Pluralities (the holding of more than one living) remained an issue for much of the century, though the practice was largely abolished by the Pluralities Act of 1838, which, with certain exceptions, limited the practice to two livings with a population of under three thousand, where the distance between the churches was less than ten miles and the joint annual income was under £1000, conditions that were further tightened by subsequent legislation.

Non-residence was another abuse only

The vicar of the parish receiving his tithes: an engraving of 1793, after the painting by Henry Singleton (1766–1839). Payment in kind could be the cause of much friction and wrangling. A character in John Dryden's opera 'King Arthur' sings: 'We've cheated the parson, we'll cheat him again, For why should a blockhead have one in ten? One in ten, one in ten?' Payment in kind was abolished by the Tithe Commutation Act of 1836, which replaced it with a rent charge on land.

16

This 'Punch' cartoon of 1895, entitled 'True Humility', was the source of the phrase 'a curate's egg', meaning something good in parts. The dialogue runs:
Right Reverend host. 'I'm afraid that you've got a bad egg, Mr Jones!'
The Curate. 'Oh no, my lord, I assure you! Parts of it are excellent!'

slowly removed, in which the incumbent lived away from the parish (inevitable in the case of pluralities) and paid a curate to perform his duties. An official return of 1827 showed that, of 10,533 benefices that responded, the incumbents of only 4413 were resident. This overstates the problem, in that the figures exclude those clergy who lived close to their churches but beyond the parish boundary, but critics made much of it. A quarter of a century later *The Times* was still complaining of non-residence:

> A man obtaining a living is instituted and inducted, read in, and then informs the Bishop that the house is too damp for him, or the church too spacious, or the parish too extensive, and he takes leave of his parish for ever; only drawing £500 a year from it, and paying £100 to his curate.

What a curate earned was a matter of private contract between him and the incumbent, although rates were laid down by law if non-resident clergymen failed to appoint, and the

The epitome of the sporting parson: the Reverend John ('Jack') Russell (1785–1883). Russell was perpetual curate of Swimbridge, Devon, from 1831 to 1880, when he became rector of Black Torrington in the same county. Best known for his breeding of the Jack Russell terrier, he performed prodigious feats on the hunting field and resisted all the efforts of Bishop Philpotts of Exeter to abolish clerical involvement in the sport.

17

Shooting and fishing, as well as hunting, were the taste of many country clergymen. 'St Partridge's Day in Our Parish' is the title of this 'Punch' cartoon of 31st August 1878. The exchange between the rector and his clerk runs:

> Sporting Rector. 'Saturday being the feast of St Enurchus, there'll be Morning Service at eleven. Tomorrow, there'll be the usual Bible meet–'
>
> Ditto Clerk (in a loud whisper). 'Houd on, pairson! Thu's forgotten t'pairtridges!'
>
> Rector (hurriedly). 'Hem! – The usual Bible meeting will not take place. Let us sing,' &c.

Right: The magic lantern was a great tool for outreach, being used in schools and Sunday schools, and for entertainment as well as education. There were many suppliers of slides of a religious character, such as views of the Holy Land. Robert Hart, vicar of Takeley, near Dunmow in Essex, wrote in his diary in 1882: 'Nov 20. To London... bought a Magic Lantern and new tea-urn for our parties.' It was soon being put to use: 'Nov 30. At 6.30 a party of 44 members of the [Dunmow Friendly Society] came to tea... so nicely managed by my dear wife; spoke to them afterwards, and then showed part of them the Magic Lantern.' (Illustration from the Catalogue of the Great Exhibition, 1851)

A member of the hunt is surprised to see the vicar out with the hounds during Lent. The clergyman explains that he is riding a 'lent horse'. The awful pun is perhaps less excusable than the hunting itself. A cartoon from 'Punch', 17th March, 1877.

HETHE RECTORY,
NEAR BICESTER.

THE EXCELLENT AND MODERN HOUSEHOLD

FURNITURE

CARPETS, CHIMNEY GLASS, HANDSOME CABINET,
BAGATELLE BOARD, GLASS, CHINA, KITCHEN REQUISITES, &c; also

A GOOD WAGONETTE, DOG CART, CARRIAGE HORSE,
FEEDING PIG,

Harness, Garden & Stable Tools, a small Stump of HAY (to go off,) and Miscellaneous Effects in and about the above Rectory,
the Property of the late Rev. F. Salter.

TO BE SOLD BY AUCTION, BY MESSRS.

JONAS PAXTON, SON, & CASTLE

ON MONDAY, AUGUST 22nd, 1881, AT ELEVEN O'CLOCK.

The parish of Hethe, near Bicester in Oxfordshire, was without a resident incumbent between 1801 and 1850. A common reason given for non-residence was lack of suitable accommodation. The sale of the rectory in 1881 gives some idea of the standard of living of a country clergyman. The comparative modesty of the house and its contents reflects a living valued at £164 in 1864. However, the late parson, Mr Salter, had owned a carriage horse, a wagonette, a dog cart – and a pig!

Bishop had to step in. In *Clergymen of the Church of England*, a collection of essays published in 1866, Anthony Trollope wrote of curates earning as little as £70 a

year, a sum below what a skilled artisan or even a senior domestic servant might expect to earn. Controversy ensued, but Trollope was vindicated, and his depiction of the Reverend Josiah Crawley, curate of Hogglestock, shows deprivations that were all too real for many.

Poor clergy, and especially curates, had an important additional source of income in the fees paid for so-called 'surplice duties', namely baptisms, weddings and funerals, without which

Writing towards the end of the nineteenth century, Richard Jefferies movingly described the plight of clergy whose charitable kindness was taken for granted by the rural poor, who showed little or no interest in the church. In this 'Punch' cartoon from 1886 a kindly parson enquires after a parishioner, during whose terminal illness he had regularly sent a can of milk. He is informed: 'He's a gone! But afore he went… he left the quart o' milk to come to me daily, poor dear!'

Regency box pews at St John's Church, Mildenhall, near Marlborough, Wiltshire. In many churches pews were rented, payment becoming due on Lady Day and Michaelmas. As church rates proved increasingly difficult to raise, so pew rents became a more crucial part of church income. Despite this, there were many opponents. John Mason Neale, the ecclesiologist and hymn writer, produced twenty-four reasons for getting rid of pews: they 'were invented by people who thought themselves too good to pray by the side of their neighbours, shut out the poor who are driven away to meeting-houses, make it impossible to pay proper attention, cause quarrels in the parish, spoil the look of a church and endanger its safety, allow parishioners to go to sleep without fear [and] harbour dust and mildew' (quoted by Owen Chadwick). Even so, pew rents survived well into the twentieth century.

many would have struggled to make ends meet. The fees could mount up. For example, in 1838 the fee income from funerals alone aggregated to £764 in St Giles-in-the-Fields, a notorious slum area of London, where death was ever present.

There was no pension to look forward to, unless the clergyman had made some provision of his own through one of a number of funds that existed. A rudimentary scheme was introduced in 1871, but a full modern scheme was not brought in until 1928–36. As old age approached, an incumbent might 'downsize' by moving to a quieter, country parish with less onerous duties. For others, the workhouse was not unknown, as was the case with the Reverend F. J. Bleasby, who in 1902 entered Tiverton workhouse, having made 470 unsuccessful applications for a curacy.

The professionalisation of the clergy

As the nineteenth century progressed, the office of clergyman became less one of amateur (though often dedicated) service by gentlemen of private means than that of a modern professional. This was part of a general trend in society and was equally evident in medicine and the law.

The growth of the professions was a remarkable feature of the Victorian period, and it affected the Church as it did other occupations. Pre-industrial society was based on an aristocratic ideal centred on property and patronage. Industrialisation was underpinned by a middle-class, entrepreneurial ideal stressing risk-taking and money-making. The rival principle of the working class, namely a collective ideal based on co-operation, was never fully achieved. An alternative middle-class ideal, stressing human capital and trained expertise, was that of the profession. It saw the

In medieval times Lammas Day (derived from 'Loaf Mass' rather than 'Lamb Mass') was a thanksgiving for the first fruits of the harvest, celebrated on 1st August. Thereafter, the religious festival fell into decline, to be replaced by a secular (and bucolic) 'Harvest Home'. Several clergymen claimed to have reintroduced the Harvest Festival, including Piers Claughton, rector of Elton, now in Cambridgeshire, and D. A. Denison, of East Brent, Somerset. The palm, however, is generally awarded to R. S. Hawker of Morwenstow in Cornwall. In 1862 the Convocation of Canterbury issued a special form of service. The illustration shows the Harvest Home at Swallowfield, near Reading, in 1863. The parish church had gained a firm grip on proceedings, which commenced with a morning service, where the church was 'filled to overflowing'. The Reverend Charles Kingsley preached. Later, some 340 labourers and their families sat down to a 'substantial repast' in a marquee, the report concluding that 'It is worthy of remark that there was not a single case of drunkenness during the day'.

Edward Monro (1815–66) came under Tractarian influence while an undergraduate at Oriel College, Oxford, but party labels were less important to him than a passionate interest in the poor. This pastoral care was shown among his rural parishioners at Harrow Weald, where he was perpetual curate between 1842 and 1860, and among the town-dwellers of the parish of St John's, Leeds, where he was vicar from 1860 until his death. He was a prolific writer and in 1850 wrote of the sensitivity that needed to be shown when visiting: 'the visits of a clergyman to his poor must lose very much force unless he lays aside the magisterial air, so very commonly used. He has no right to cross the poor man's threshold with a covered head, nor in any degree to demean himself as a superior within the walls of the cottage.' The social divide between clergyman and parishioners is evident in this engraving from 'The Cottager' of 1862. The Reverend Sabine Baring-Gould, rector and squire of Lew Trenchard in Devon from 1881 until his death in 1924, regularly did his visiting by carriage, though he did give advance warning of his intention to call.

professional as a person of trust, in whom was vested a monopoly of socially valuable knowledge. Being removed from vulgar money-making, the professions enjoyed a higher social status, for aristocratic ideas lingered on. Henry Byerly Thomson was a barrister, and the son of a physician. In 1857 he wrote, in his book *The Choice of a Profession*:

The member of the higher professions... at once takes a place in society by virtue of his calling; the poor man of business is nowhere in social position, yet the poor curate is admitted readily to that coveted country society that the millionaire has even to manoeuvre for.

There was some truth in his claim. When, in Trollope's novel *The Last Chronicle of Barset* (1867), Archdeacon Grantly greets the poverty-stricken

An advertisement from the 'London Diocesan Book', 1882. There were countless publishers of religious tracts, and many clergy maintained a stock to distribute when visiting. The most prolific publisher was the Religious Tract Society. Established in 1799, it had a committee composed of an equal number of Anglicans and Nonconformists, an example of the way that evangelicalism could cross denominational boundaries. Millions of tracts were distributed in the nineteenth century, either by colporteurs (hawkers), by clergymen or by enthusiastic lay people.

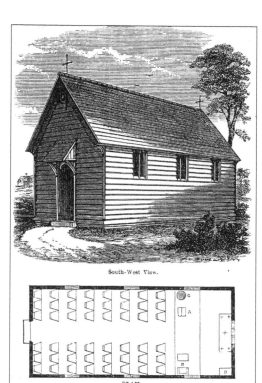

South-West View.

PLAN.
A Lectern. B Reading-desk. C Stove. D Credence.
Hamlet Chapel, for 60 adults, for £100.

Design for a hamlet mission church to accommodate sixty adults, for a cost of £100, from 'The Church Builder', 1875. Before 1850 there was both suspicion and legal objection to holding services elsewhere than the parish church. Outdoor preaching, with its associations with Methodism, was considered particularly scandalous. In order to reach out to their parishioners, some clergy offered 'lectures' in the village schoolroom. In 1855 the Evangelical Lord Shaftesbury secured amendment to the law that had prohibited the meeting for worship of more than twenty people except in church or licensed dissenting chapels. This opened the way for the erection of mission churches and halls, which seem to have been pioneered in Lincolnshire, where, in 1857, a mission hall was erected in the parish of Tydd St Mary, which was 12 miles in length. The conduct of services in such buildings was often assigned to lay readers, an office created in 1865. There was a great reluctance to give lay readers a share in leading worship in the church itself, and as late as 1904 they were allowed to preach in the churches of only four dioceses.

Sidney Godolphin Osborne (1808–89) was an aristocrat, whose family background gave him the strength to push for social reform against the determined opposition of vested interests. He was rector of Stoke Poges, Buckinghamshire, from 1832 to 1841, and of Durweston, Dorset, from 1841 to 1875. It was there that he did important work fighting to improve the condition of the agricultural labourer. His main weapon was a series of 'lay sermons' delivered through the correspondence columns of 'The Times', under the signature 'S.G.O.' (which his admirers interpreted as 'Sincere, Good and Outspoken'). His concerns were widespread and encompassed sanitation, education, cholera and women's rights. Brother-in-law of Charles Kingsley, Osborne held that it was the duty of the church to 'preach the plain truth boldly, that God will not have the poor oppressed in body or in spirit'.

The clergy played a crucial role in elementary education. In 1847 the National Society, which was the Church of England's body for promoting parish schools, reported that the quality of parochial education depended largely on the extent to which the incumbent was willing and able to finance the running of the school. As well as raising finance, local clergy visited schools, where they (and their wives) might occasionally teach. Clergymen also acted as Her Majesty's Inspectors of Education, for under a concordat agreed with the Archbishops of Canterbury and York in 1840 inspectors of Church of England Schools were invariably ordained. (Engraving from 'The Victoria Picture Spelling Book' of 1872)

perpetual curate of Hogglestock in his library, he is able to say, despite his visitor's worn clothing and battered boots, 'We stand on the only perfect level on which such men can meet each other. We are both gentlemen.'

A profession was an occupation for a gentleman, and anyone from a lower social position raised his status on entry. Professional status depended on a monopoly (enforceable by law) of an area of sought-after knowledge, with practitioners able to regulate entry into their ranks and to discipline their members. As professions jockeyed for position, they not only acquired new roles but were forced to give up others that were now claimed by rivals. In the early nineteenth century clergy roles embraced not only those of leader of worship, preacher and celebrant of the Sacraments, but also secular roles such as almoner, officer of law and order, educator, officer of health and politician. In the early decades of the nineteenth century, for example, clergy continued to provide much medical treatment, often running their own dispensaries. But as the medical profession became more organised, doctors became less tolerant. For example, in 1862 the Reverend Francis Cunningham, rector of East Tisted, near Alton in Hampshire, where smallpox, scarlet fever and typhoid raged, was reprimanded by a local doctor for visiting infectious cases and changing dressings.

In the early years of the century, clergy, if not themselves gentry by origin, had grown close to the squirearchy and took a full part in county business. In 1813, for example, soon after his ordination, Charles Blomfield (later Bishop of London) wrote to a friend that he had become a justice of the peace and a commissioner of turnpikes and was likely to become a commissioner for the property tax. With the property qualification for magistrates raised in 1774 from £40 to £100, in some areas the clergyman might be one of very few people qualified. The clergy also seem to have made very good magistrates, for they were well educated and not open to corruption.

Over 36 per cent of the Oxfordshire bench of magistrates were clergy in 1816, falling to 21 per cent in 1857. Many clergy could see that their secular activities might conflict with their essential professional role. The writer John Sterling (died 1844) wrote that parsons were 'black dragoons' in the villages, and that to be seen as agents of the law (and protectors of property) damaged their relationship with poor parishioners. Matters came to a head in 1873, when two local rectors, sitting on the bench at Chipping Norton, sent sixteen women to prison for intimidating blackleg labourers during a farmworkers' strike. An unsuccessful attempt was made to bring in legislation banning clergymen from the bench (as they had been banned from becoming Members of Parliament in 1801), but numbers fell by themselves. By 1906 there were only thirty-two clerical magistrates left.

The social influence of the clergyman yet remained tremendous. A good reference from the vicar could secure a young girl or boy a job, and there were many legal documents requiring the signature of a person of standing such as a clergyman. There was a reluctance to offend the local vicar, who was often the fount of charity. When the squire and the vicar were the same person (the 'squarson') there were even greater opportunities for clerical pressure on parishioners. At Bloxworth, in Dorset, for example, where the Reverend Octavius Pickard-Cambridge took over from his father as rector in 1868, if a labourer missed attendance at church on one or two Sundays, the threat hung over him that he would lose his cottage. Many clergy rightly saw such pressure as malign, but some even saw benign parochial intervention as interfering with the spiritual relationship that ought to exist between a pastor and his flock. That intervention took many forms, from the inauguration and implementation of savings clubs and clothing clubs, the provision

While the Anglican and Nonconformist churches undoubtedly spread elementary education in the nineteenth century, interdenominational rivalry also checked the ability of the State to complete the system. This 'Punch' cartoon dates from 1852.

of food supplements to the infirm and elderly, and the establishment (often on part or all of their glebe land) of allotments to enable labourers to provide a better diet for themselves. The strain on many clergymen was considerable, for they had to be all things to all men. There was the risk of antagonising local employers, who might object to time-consuming allotments and the independence these gave, while clerical support of trade unions was anathema to many. On the other side, many working people accepted material help, while rejecting all spiritual teaching.

The gradual withdrawal from secular roles enabled the clergy to concentrate on those professional activities to which they could with justification claim a monopoly, namely their priestly duties of leading worship, preaching and, particularly, the celebration of the Sacraments. The church building increasingly came to be seen as the locus of this activity, and hence there developed an interest both in church restoration and in the minutiae of worship and liturgy. Both Evangelicals and Tractarians came to see the clergyman as one set apart and consecrated for specific duties. The Tractarians emphasised the importance of the Sacraments, claiming authority through apostolic succession. Not only were churches restored, but the focal point within many of them moved from the pulpit to the altar. There were other trends leading to a greater emphasis on the Sacraments. The introduction of civil registration in 1836 had a knock-on effect. Previously baptism, recorded in the church register, gave a child legal existence. With civil registration, this was no longer the case, and so clergy came to lay stress on the sacramental nature of the event.

Over the century, then, the professional role of the clergy became focused. Secular activities were thrown off, and the priestly role was enhanced. As the clergy grew

An advertisement of 1878 for Bethany House School, the great aim of which was 'to prepare youths for commercial and business pursuits, and to train them in the fear of the Lord, which is the beginning of wisdom'. There were hundreds of such schools catering for the needs of the middle class. Many were small, and many were run by clergymen, either alongside parochial duties or as a sole career. Indeed, the higher social status enjoyed by teachers in secondary (i.e. middle-class) schools compared with those in elementary schools was partly derived from the fact that so many of them were ordained clergy.

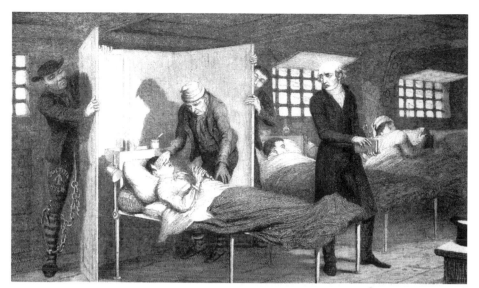

An engraving from George Cruikshank's series 'The Drunkard's Children', published in 1848. The drunkard's son is sentenced to transportation for life but dies on the prison hulk 'Justitia', as the chaplain looks on. Prisons, poor law hospitals, asylums and other institutions provided employment for many clergymen in the nineteenth century.

apart from other professions, so they grew closer to each other. Clergy meetings became more frequent, with rural deaneries being re-established in the mid 1830s. Diocesan synods were revived, and Convocation, the ancient provincial assembly of the Church of England, which had not been called since 1771, was revived in 1852 (Canterbury) and 1861 (York). Railways made all this possible. Bishop William Stubbs (1825–1901) once asked a group of high-school girls:

'What book beginning with a B has a bishop to study the most?'
'The Bible?'
'No, Bradshaw [the railway timetable guide]!'

A professional culture developed, and within it distinct sub-cultures. Nowhere were these more to be seen than in relation to liturgy.

Worship, preaching and liturgy

In the Church of England the clergyman enjoyed a monopoly of leading worship, a right maintained both by canon and statute law. The minimum required, which came to be known as 'the duty', was the reading of Morning and Evening Prayer on Sunday. Practice varied, but in the eighteenth century the morning service had generally consisted of Morning Prayer, followed by the Litany and Ante-Communion, and a sermon. The evening service was generally held in the afternoon, so that people could return home before dark, and consisted of Evening Prayer, sometimes with a second sermon. This left a gap of about two hours between services, which was filled with the performance of baptisms, churchings, marriages and burials. If 'the duty' was the minimum, it went the way of all minima and became the norm. Weekday services were at first rare. A large portion of Sunday duty was performed by curates for a single-duty fee, and 'gallopers' (curates riding from one church to another in order to officiate) were quite common. Charlotte Yonge recalled that at Otterburn, in North Yorkshire, at the end of the

"WHO SAYS THERE IS NOT A SURPLICE!"

THE SURPLICE QUESTION.

BY A BENEDICT.

A VERY pretty public stir
Is making, down at Exeter,
About the surplice fashion:
And many bitter words and rude
Have been bestow'd upon the feud,
And much unchristian passion.

For me, I neither know nor care
Whether a Parson ought to wear
A black dress or a white dress;
Fill'd with a trouble of my own,—
A Wife who preaches in her gown,
And lectures in her night-dress!

In the winter of 1844–5 there were riots in Exeter over the wearing of the surplice while preaching. Canon 74 of the Church of England, on 'Decency of Apparel enjoined to Ministers', had laid down the use of the gown, and the black preaching gown was de rigeur among Evangelical Anglicans. Puritans had described the surplice as 'a fool's coat' and 'a rag of the whore of Babylon'. By the beginning of the nineteenth century the surplice was often regarded as quaint and old-fashioned, but it lingered on in rural parishes. Gradually it was reintroduced, but not always without opposition. After the parishioners of Helston, in Cornwall, complained about their priest preaching in a surplice, in November 1844 Bishop Philpotts of Exeter (Cornwall at that time being in his diocese) issued a pastoral letter requiring the use of the surplice when preaching. Reaction was so strong that he was forced to withdraw the order a month later, making the issue one of individual discretion. When the Reverend Francis Courtenay, perpetual curate of St Sidwell's in Exeter, continued to use the surplice, which his predecessor had reintroduced, there were riots, which lasted over three Sundays in January 1845 and drew crowds of up to five thousand people. It took decades for the question to die down, but the surplice was accepted in most churches by the 1870s. By then there were other matters of sartorial dispute, especially over vestments worn at Holy Communion. This punning engraving and poem are from 'Hood's Own', edited by Thomas Hood.

28

REYNOLDS, RICHARDS, & CO.,
CLERICAL HATTERS,
15, WELLINGTON STREET, STRAND, W.C.
(NEAR WATERLOO BRIDGE).

ESTABLISHED 1826.

ALL GOODS OF THE BEST QUALITY.

(1)
Soft Crown, 3 in. deep,
3 in. stiff brim, price 12/6.

Dignitaries'
Hat.

(2)
Soft Crown, 3 in. deep,
3 in. stiff brim, price 10/6.

(3)
Soft Felt, 4½ in. deep,
3 in. brim, price 10/6.

(4)
Dignitaries' Soft Felt,
price 11/6.

(5)
Stiff Felt, 4½ in. deep,
3 in. brim, price 12/6.

(6)
Soft Felt, 3½ in. deep, brims,
3. 3½, and 4 in., price 9/6.

Plain Dress Hat,
12/6, 16/6, 20/-

(7)
Soft Felt, 5 in. deep,
3½ in. brim, price 9/6.

(8)
Soft Felt, 5 in. deep,
3 in. brim, price 10/6.

College Caps,
from 42/- per dozen.*
* Black Tassels, from 9d. each. Coloured ditto, from 1/6 each.

(9)
Soft Felt, 4 in. deep,
3 in. brim, price 9/6.

Scull Cap, Silk, 5/6.

Scull Cap, Velvet, 7/6.

Directions for Self-Measurement: —
Inches round the Head, and Length and Breadth of Hat in Wear.

A selection of clerical hats from an advertisement in 'A Kalendar of the English Church and Ecclesiastical Almanack' of 1882. The commonest styles among the lower clergy were the shallow-crowned and broad-rimmed hat, and the plain dress hat. Dignitaries' hats had brims supported by cords, as seen also in the photograph of T. W. Drury, who became the fourth Bishop of Ripon in 1911.

eighteenth century the bells summoning people to morning worship were not rung until the curate's horse could be seen approaching in the distance.

Even though laid down, the afternoon service was often omitted, with a consequent impact on church attendance, for many people (farm workers and domestic servants, for example) had duties that made a choice of times necessary. The Evangelicals took a more serious view, and by the 1830s there was a general trend to increase the number of services. The Oxford Movement had a similar impact. St Peter's, London Docks, for example, had six Sunday services by the 1860s.

The sermon has often been considered the touchstone of a parson's performance, and it is difficult to generalise about the quality of Victorian preaching. The Church of England was blessed with many fine preachers, but the observation of the Reverend C. Suttell, in his book *Preachers and Preaching* (1888), may not be far from the mark:

Whoever has noticed the character of the preaching most common throughout Christendom at the present time, is aware that what they *generally* hear is either the droning, uninstructive, inefficient essay; or the polished and pleasant, but utterly pointless

Thomas Pratt & Sons were proud of their 'Pocket Surplice' in its neat leather case, and they advertised it widely. This advertisement comes from a church almanac of 1868. The biretta, widely worn by Roman Catholic clergy, was confined to High Church clergymen in the Church of England. Towards the end of the nineteenth century attempts were made to revive the square cap of black cloth, as more suitable for Anglicans.

exhortation; or the impassioned, fire and brimstone harangue; or, which is perhaps more unsuited to the pulpit than any other kind of discourse, some common-place, desultory extempore (unpremeditated) address filled up with vulgar anecdotes and supposed witty sayings.

A country clergyman once asked an applicant for the reading of banns of marriage: 'Do you sleep in the parish?' The reply was not the expected one. 'Yes, sir, I have slept through several of your sermons.' The narcotic effect was no doubt increased by the fact that sermons were usually read. They were often ones that the preacher had recycled, either from his own compositions or from those of others. There were many sources of sermon outlines. The Reverend Charles Simeon (1759–1836), the Evangelical divine, published 2536 outlines in twenty-one volumes. Published sermons still involved the labour of transcription, though not for those who employed the services of the Reverend John Trusler (1735–1820). He had the ingenuity to publish 150 sermons engraved in imitation of handwriting, and available at one shilling each, an enterprise that proved a real money-spinner for him.

The service that underwent the greatest change was Holy Communion. In the eighteenth century Holy Communion was infrequent, and three times a year was the norm. In 1800, even at Easter (the supreme Christian festival), there was only one

30

Mrs Little advertised her Ecclesiastical Warehouse in Debrett's 'Illustrated Peerage' of 1867. One of her selling points was that she provided 'all Materials for Ladies' own working'. Not everyone approved of such arrangements. Percy Dearmer was ordained priest in 1892 and wrote 'The Parson's Handbook' in 1899. From 1901 to 1906 he was first Professor of Ecclesiastical Art at King's College London. He wrote with passion on the dangers of allowing well-meaning ladies to prettify vestments: 'The parson will… use a gentle authority against the good ladies who unconsciously try to approximate church vestments to the feminine attire with which they are familiar. For ecclesiastical vestments are for men, and it will be a bad day for us when we forget this fact.'

celebration of Communion at St Paul's Cathedral, with only six communicants. The influence of the Oxford Movement in the 1830s and 1840s led to much greater frequency, and by the middle decades of the century monthly Holy Communion had become the norm throughout England, with weekly Communion services largely confined to churches with a Tractarian parson. For the Tractarians the ritual aspects of the service assumed great importance and led to some of the most visible divisions within the Church of England. Writing at the very end of the century, Percy Dearmer observed that:

The Archbishop of Canterbury, in a recent charge at Maidstone, has pointed out that, though the Church of England wisely allows a certain amount of doctrinal

Finer points of ritual were frequently lost on members of the congregation, whose main concern, as ever, was often that things should stay as they were. The exchange in this 'Punch' cartoon, from January 1872, runs:

High Church Curate. 'And what do you think, Mr Simpson, about a clergyman's turning to the east?'

Literal Churchwarden: 'Well, sir, my opinion is, that if the clergyman is goodlookin', he don't want to turn his back to the congregation!'

31

latitude to her clergy, she is very strict as to ceremonial... nothing more enthusiastic than 'assent' is required to the [Thirty-nine] Articles, but the undertaking as to the forms of public prayer admits of no compromise... The ceremonial stands before us as the order of the Church. The teaching is, and must be to a very large extent, the voice of the individual. The ceremonial is for all alike.

The founders of the Oxford Movement were very conservative in all aspects of public ceremonial, but their stress on placing the Church of England within the broader Catholic tradition was bound to lead others to wish to restore catholic (though not necessarily Roman Catholic) ritual. For many clergy, especially those working among the urban poor, there was an evangelistic aspect to ceremonial. Vestments and the use of candles and incense added to the sense of awe, and the light and colour brought home the majesty of the service. It was argued that, through the senses, ritualism reached those to whom oral instruction presented problems. A medieval idea seemed fitted to the modern age.

However, to those who concerned themselves with such matters, ritual acts (such as the position taken by the priest at the altar when celebrating Communion) conveyed subtle theological differences, and those opposed to ritualistic changes fought relentlessly against them. In 1865 several leading Evangelicals formed the Church Association to maintain the Protestant ideals of the Church of England.

The use of the cross for ornamentation or as a ritualistic symbol was a matter of much controversy in the 1870s. Sabine Baring-Gould's great hymn 'Onward, Christian Soldiers', now unfashionable because it is held by some to be tainted with militarism, was scorned by nineteenth-century Low Churchmen because of its line 'With the cross of Jesus going on before', an allusion, some held, to non-canonical processions. In this 'Punch' cartoon from 1878 the Tractarian parson assures a suspicious churchwarden that no cross has been added to the reading desk. Indeed, as he points out, one has been taken away. The clergyman is wearing the clothes favoured by advanced Tractarians, including the long, buttoned coat known to detractors as an 'MB coat'. This stood for 'Mark of the Beast', and probably originated in tailors' shorthand.

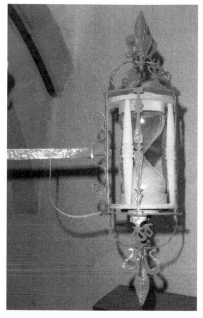

An hourglass at Compton Bassett, Wiltshire. Hourglasses were still used in some nineteenth-century churches and may have prevented some long sermons from being even longer. In 1899 the Reverend Percy Dearmer wrote: 'The congregation will often have come to be grateful if there is a clock within sight of the pulpit.' According to Elizabeth Gaskell, the Reverend Patrick Brontë, at Haworth, West Yorkshire, could preach a perfectly timed thirty-minute sermon, even when blind.

Nicknamed the 'Persecution Society' by its opponents, it later boasted of having spent £80,000 in litigation, and to have obtained sixty legal judgements against ritualists.

These cases highlighted the difficulties that existed over matters of church discipline. While bishops had disciplinary powers over the clergy of their dioceses, in practice these proved remarkably difficult to enforce. The ultimate sanction was deprivation, or the taking away from a clergyman of his benefice or ecclesiastical preferment. There were many grounds for this, ranging from incorrigible drunkenness and gross immorality to maintaining doctrines derogatory to the Thirty-nine Articles or the Book of Common Prayer. But the clergyman had a right of appeal, which, after 1834, stretched ultimately to the Judicial Committee of the Privy Council. This was a secular court, and it was anathema to many in the Church of England that questions of doctrine should be decided by a secular authority. Thus, for example, though in 1871 and 1877 the Judicial Committee of the Privy Council condemned vestments as illegal, the statistics show that the decisions had little impact, for the use of vestments not only continued but spread. The heat generated by controversies over ritual led eventually to the passage (much to the delight of Queen Victoria) of the Public Worship Regulation Act of 1874, to provide simpler procedures for correcting certain ecclesiastical offences. Though not repealed until 1963, it proved largely unworkable. The imprisonment of four Anglican priests for contumacy between 1877 and 1889 merely created martyrs. Ironically, an important legacy of the Act was to increase the influence and the authority of the bishops as guides to the clergy on what was reasonable agreement with the rubrics and what was acceptable liturgical experiment.

By 1900 worship was very different from a century before. Richard Jefferies wrote of the changes discernible in the country church:

There were brazen candlesticks behind the altar, and beautiful flowers. Before, the interior was all black and white. Now there was a sense of colour. The place was lit up with a new light. After the first revolt of the old folk there was little opposition, because the vicar, being a man who had studied human nature and full of practical wisdom as well as learning, did all things gradually. (From *Hodge and His Masters*, 1880.)

33

A fashionable wedding at St James's, Piccadilly; from George Augustus Sala, 'Twice Round the Clock', 1859. In the eighteenth century weddings had generally been performed on Sunday, but by the middle of the nineteenth century clergy showed a general preference for weekdays. This was partly due to the multiplication of Sunday services, but also because Evangelicals frowned upon Sunday marriages on account of the jollities that accompanied them.

Town church and cathedral close

Much of what we have looked at so far relates particularly to country clergymen. But what of those who lived and worked in the towns? Urbanisation was a phenomenon of the nineteenth century, with the 1851 Census revealing that for the first time more people in England and Wales were living in towns than in the countryside. Not all towns were new, of course, nor were they all industrial. There were many ancient boroughs and these included the cathedral cities. This last section, therefore, looks at clergy facing the problems of large urban parishes and those enjoying the quietness of the cathedral close.

Anthony Trollope chronicled the life of the cathedral close in his Barsetshire novels, but he also had observations to make on the town clergy. In his book *Clergymen of the Church of England* (1866) he observed: 'The town incumbent... is rarely a man well to do in the world. He is one who earns his bread hardly in the sweat of his brow, and too often earns but very poor bread.' Whereas in the country the parson was all but equal to the squire, the town parson was not equal to the town mayor. As Trollope put it, 'he is too often simply recognised as the professional gentleman who has taken his family into the last built new house in Albert Terrace'. His relationship with his parishioners was likely to be less intimate. Trollope makes the point that the town church is perhaps better described as a 'place of worship' than as a parish church, for urban congregations were likely to be less settled. With

The Reverend Arthur Jephson, of St John's, Walworth, in London, conducts a batch wedding of ten couples in about 1900. He had joined eight thousand couples in matrimony, sometimes in groups of up to forty-five couples at a time. Such a practice was not illegal, though by this time it was largely discontinued. So-called 'penny weddings' had been a means by which the poor could marry without paying a full 'surplice fee'. The officiant needed to stay alert, however. The Reverend Joshua Brookes, eccentric chaplain of the Collegiate Church, Manchester, in the early nineteenth century, once got all the pairings wrong. 'Sort yourselves when you go out' was his response.

the probability that there would be other places of worship (including other Anglican churches) to choose from, the clergyman became subject to market forces. 'Those who want him', Trollope insisted, 'will come to him and pay him, as they do to the baker or the dentist.' The popular preacher would draw the crowds, the pews would be full, and the pew rents would increase the parson's income.

This was perhaps true of middle-class congregations. The great challenge to the church was reaching the masses. There were many clergymen who made this task their life's work, with greater or lesser success. Often they were of the High Church persuasion, convinced that the sights and sounds (as well as the smells) of High Church worship were attractive to working people, whose own lives had little that was of beauty. The real attraction, however, may have been the charismatic personalities of the clergy themselves – men like Arthur Stanton, once described as the most influential curate in the history of the Church of England, or Samuel Barnett, the founder of Toynbee Hall, a settlement in east London. Stanton loved the poor and when he was dying gave £10 to be distributed solely among the *undeserving*. The demand for charitable help from the Church was enormous. Canon Barnett, when vicar of St Jude's, Whitechapel, was besieged by desperate

The Reverend Wilson Carlile (1847–1942) inherited a family silk business, which was ruined by economic recession. In 1881 he was ordained priest, and he dedicated his life to working with the urban poor. He founded the Church Army, which was essentially staffed by members of the laity. In 1897 Convocation established the office of evangelist. At first only men were commissioned; women had to wait until 1921. Carlile was a prebendary of St Paul's from 1906 to 1942 and was created a Companion of Honour in 1926.

35

William Howley (1766–1848) was appointed Archbishop of Canterbury in 1828. He is shown here wearing the rochet and chimere prescribed by canon law for the use of bishops. The rochet is a full-length robe made of the finest cotton or linen lawn, with the voluminous sleeves gathered at the wrist with a frill. The chimere is the gown of black or scarlet that is worn over the rochet, scarlet being reserved technically (though not always in practice) for those bishops who were also doctors of divinity. Howley is wearing the clerical wig, which many early nineteenth-century bishops wished to dispense with, a move to which George IV would never give his assent. John Bird Sumner, Archbishop of Canterbury between 1848 and 1862, was the last cleric to wear the episcopal wig.

men demanding help and had to have an escape door cut through the church wall, so that he could summon help.

All this was very different from the cathedral close. The cathedral is the church that contains the 'throne' (Latin *cathedra*) of the bishop of a diocese. In early times the cathedral, being close to the bishop's palace, was served by the bishop himself, but as his administrative duties within the diocese became more onerous, and as the services of the cathedral became more elaborate, responsibility for the cathedral itself passed to a separate ecclesiastical body, the chapter, presided over by the dean. The chapter consisted of a number of residentiary canons, plus a larger body of non-resident canons known as prebendaries. Readers of Trollope's Barchester novels will be familiar with the sheltered lives of many cathedral clergy.

The American writer Ralph Waldo Emerson marvelled at the way bishops were appointed within the established Church of England:

> The Bishop is elected by the Dean and Prebends of the cathedral. The Queen sends these gentlemen a *congé d'elire*, or leave to elect; but also sends them the name of the person whom they are to elect. They go into the cathedral, chant and pray, and

An engraving, after the painting by Sir George Hayter, of the baptism of the Prince of Wales in January 1842. Archbishop Howley tended to become flustered on royal occasions, and there was some trepidation lest he drop the baby. Writing half a century later, the Reverend Percy Dearmer offered this advice: 'If [the priest] be inexperienced, he should ask some woman to instruct him in the proper manner of holding babies; it is really important, both for the sake of the parents, and for that of quietness, that he should be handy with children.'

A confirmation of boys from Westminster School in Westminster Abbey. This engraving by Gustave Doré is from 'London: A Pilgrimage', published in 1872. Doré is best known for his engravings of London slums, and their harsh lines and dark forms are in marked contrast to the lightness of his touch when depicting the fashionable West End. His collaborator, Blanchard Jerrold, wrote: 'These lads — the flower of the country whose paths tend to the senate and the council chamber, and who will be among the future governors of the Empire; are ranged and gowned... The bishop lays his hands upon their sunny, comely heads. It is a day and time of high hopes that stir the imagination vividly.'

beseech the Holy Ghost to assist them in their choice; and after these invocations invariably find the dictates of the Holy Ghost agree with the recommendations of the Queen.

The Queen was herself bound by the advice of her Prime Minister, and the composition of the bench of bishops depended much on how seriously he took the task, and how fixed were his own religious views. Lord Palmerston, for example, took advice from his son-in-law Lord Shaftesbury, who worked hard to ensure Evangelical supremacy. The Queen was for

The church fête or bazaar has become a fixture in the English calendar, especially in rural areas. However, such events aroused strong feelings in the nineteenth century, for, while some clergymen saw their necessity in raising needed funds, others considered them an inappropriate way for the church to finance parochial activities. They were one of the ways in which women could participate in church activities, patronising though this seems today. In this 'Punch' cartoon of 1886, the Dean is surrounded by female admirers, but the 'Fair Stranger' is asking the price of the frame without the photograph.

The Missions to Seamen Society was formed in 1857. By 1878 it had thirty-six honorary chaplains, thirteen mission clergymen, twenty-five Scripture readers and two lay helpers. This engraving from 'The Graphic' of 30th January 1878 shows a service on the church ship (an old converted frigate), moored on the river Tyne. 'The church ship serves as a parsonage for the chaplain, and for his Scripture reader, a house for the boats used in pastoral visitation on the river, a reading room and museum ever open to the sailor, a lecture room on week nights, and a "house of prayer" literally "for all nations" and languages, on the Sunday.'

Broad Churchmen and scholars and, left to herself, would have excluded both Tractarians and extreme Evangelicals. Theoretically, she had the right of veto, which, paradoxically, increased the influence of the Archbishop of Canterbury, hitherto often bypassed in the process of selection. Both Prime Minister and Queen came more and more to seek his views in order to be sure of their ground.

As the century progressed, bishops became increasingly efficient at managing what could be an enormous workload. Samuel Wilberforce, when Bishop of Oxford from 1845 to 1869, wrote forty letters a day and was responsible for building one hundred churches, seventy parsonage houses and a theological college. The spread of the railways was an enormous boon, greatly affecting the practice of confirmation, for example. In the eighteenth century it was commonplace for bishops to confirm in the market towns of their dioceses only once in three years, with vast numbers of candidates dealt with in a cursory manner. More frequent and more intimate confirmations gave that rite the sacramental significance it deserved.

Whether bishops, vicars or humble curates, the Victorian clergy have an honourable place in the history of the Church of England, and their legacy endures. They built or restored many of the churches used by today's worshippers; they wrote hymns of enduring quality; and they provided for many social needs before the modern state took over that role. They were not without their faults, but they were creatures of their age and should be judged by that alone.

Further reading

Armstrong, Patrick. *The English Parson-Naturalist*. Gracewing, 2000.

Barrow, Andrew. *The Flesh Is Weak: An Intimate History of the Church of England*. Hamish Hamilton, 1980.

Bullock, F. W. B. *A History of Training for the Ministry of the Church of England in England and Wales from 1800 to 1870*. Budd & Gillatt, 1955.

Chadwick, Owen. *The Victorian Church*. A. & C. Black, Part One 1966, Part Two 1970.

Chapman, Raymond. *Godly and Righteous, Peevish and Perverse. Clergy and Religious in Literature and Letters: An Anthology*. William B. Eerdmans, 2002.

Clark, G. Kitson. *Churchmen and the Condition of England, 1832–1885*. Methuen, 1973.

Colloms, Brenda. *Victorian Country Parsons*. Constable, 1977.

Davies, E. W. L. *The Out-of-Doors Life of the Revd. John Russell*. Richard Bentley & Son, 1883.

Davies, Horton. *Worship and Theology in England, from Watts and Wesley to Martineau, 1690–1900*. William B. Eerdmans, 1996.

Dearmer, Percy. *The Parson's Handbook*. Grant Richards, 1899.

Ditchfield, P. H. *The Old Time Parson*. Methuen, 1909.

Hart, A. Tindal. *Some Clerical Oddities in the Church of England from Mediaeval to Modern Times*. New Horizon, 1980.

Hart, A. Tindal, and Carpenter, Edward. *The Nineteenth Century Country Parson*. Wilding & Son, 1954.

Hinton, Michael. *The Anglican Parochial Clergy*. SCM Press, 1994.

Jay, Elizabeth. *Faith and Doubt in Victorian Britain*. Macmillan, 1986.

Jefferies, Richard. *Hodge and His Masters*. First published 1880; reprinted, Alan Sutton, 1992.

Kilvert, Francis. *Kilvert's Diary, 1870–79: Selections from the Diary of the Rev. Francis Kilvert* (with an introduction by William Plomer). Pimlico, 1999.

Mayo, Janet. *A History of Ecclesiastical Dress*. Batsford, 1984.

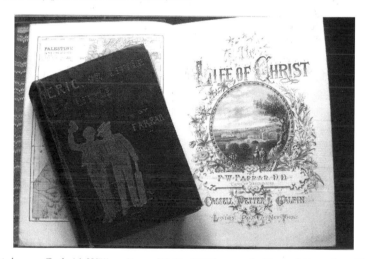

After a varied career, Frederick William Farrar (1831–1903) rose to be Dean of Canterbury. He taught at Harrow School for fifteen years, before becoming headmaster of Marlborough College. From there he went to Westminster, where he was both a canon and rector of nearby St Margaret's Church. He took his parish responsibilities seriously and was particularly concerned over the drunkenness prevalent in the Westminster slums. Farrar is less well known now than he was in his day, though frequenters of second-hand bookshops are likely to turn up his many books, such as 'Eric, or Little by Little', a public-school tale second only to 'Tom Brown's Schooldays' in its popularity. More significant was his 'Life of Christ', completed in 1874 and running to thirty editions in his lifetime. Farrar was interested in scientific discoveries and in new scholarship in several fields, including philology (where he took an evolutionary approach to language) and biblical studies. He was largely responsible for ensuring Charles Darwin's burial in Westminster Abbey (a decision that was not unchallenged) and he acted as one of the pall-bearers.

McClatchey, Diane. *Oxfordshire Clergy, 1777–1869*. Clarendon Press, 1960.

Russell, Anthony. *The Clerical Profession*. SPCK, 1980.

Suttell, C. *Preachers and Preaching*. Guardian Office, Brighton, 1888.

Towler, Robert, and Coxon, A. P. M. *The Fate of the Anglican Clergy*. Macmillan, 1979.

Trollope, Anthony. *Clergymen of the Church of England*. First published 1866; reprinted, Leicester University Press, 1974.

Whitehead, Benjamin. *Church Law*. Stevens & Sons, 1899.

Wilson, A. N. *The Faber Book of Church and Clergy*. Faber, 1992.

Helpful books in church visiting are:

Fewins, Clive. *The Church Explorer's Handbook*. Canterbury Press, 2005. Supported by The Open Churches Trust, this describes more than a thousand churches worth visiting in England, Scotland and Wales.

Friar, Stephen. *The Companion to the English Parish Church*. Alan Sutton, 1996. This book is very comprehensive and covers church history as well as architecture.

Pevsner, Niklaus, et al. *The Buildings of England* (series). Penguin.

Useful websites

The Church of England website (www.cofe.anglican.org) is useful for making comparisons with the contemporary Church and has links to many other sites.

Lambeth Palace Library's site (www.lambethpalacelibrary.org) contains excellent bibliographical material and is especially useful for genealogists.

The Clergy of the Church of England Database is an ongoing research database of clergy between 1540 and 1835. It will be found at www.theclergydatabase.org.uk

Places to visit

Although there are museums containing material relevant to the Victorian clergyman, the best places to start are often churches themselves, and not just nineteenth-century ones. The Victorian parson served in churches from every previous period of English history and altered many of them in accordance with contemporary ideas of liturgy and aesthetics. A good starting point is always the list of vicars or rectors that hangs in most churches. These first appeared in the early 1880s and were much encouraged by Archbishop Benson, who applauded them as a sign of both the continuity and the catholicity of the Church of England. These lists give a sense of the long service of many Victorian clergy, as well as the power of family patronage. The Reverend Bartholomew Edwards, for example, was rector of Ashill in Norfolk for almost seventy-six years. At Kilkhampton in Cornwall there were only four incumbents between 1804 and 1940. As one of these stayed only two years, the average service of the other three was around forty-five years. At Rosehill, near South Molton, Devon, eight generations of the Southcombe family were incumbents between 1675 and 1949.

The following list includes several places associated with particular clergy and two museums located in former bishop's palaces. Visitors are advised to check the times and dates of opening before travelling. In addition, many county and local museums have displays on religion in their areas.

Brontë Parsonage Museum, Church Street, Haworth, Keighley, West Yorkshire BD22 8DR.
  Telephone: 01535 642323. Website: www.bronte.info

Carmarthen Museum, Abergwili, Carmarthen, Carmarthenshire SA31 2JG.
  Telephone: 01267 228696. Website: www.carmarthenmuseum.org.uk.
  The museum is housed in a building that was the palace of the Bishops of St David's from 1542 to 1974.

Carrow House Costume and Textile Study Centre, 301 King Street, Norwich, Norfolk NR1 2TS.
  Telephone: 01603 223870. For ecclesiastical costume. This is a study centre rather than a museum. Anyone may use it, and it is open on Tuesdays and Thursdays. Telephone to arrange a visit, for which up to three weeks notice may be required.

Cowper and Newton Museum, Orchard Side, Market Place, Olney, Buckinghamshire MK46 4AJ.
  Telephone: 01234 711516. Website: www.cowperandnewtonmuseum.org.uk Contains material relating to the Evangelical Reverend John Newton, former slave trader and author of 'Amazing Grace'.

Epworth Old Rectory, 1 Rectory Street, Epworth, North Lincolnshire DN9 1HX.
  Telephone: 01427 872268. Website: www.epwortholdrectory.org.uk Boyhood home of John Wesley, founder of Methodism, and of Charles Wesley, his Anglican hymn-writing brother.

Fulham Palace and Museum, Bishop's Avenue, Fulham, London SW6 6EA.
  Telephone: 020 7736 3233. Former home of the Bishops of London.

Gilbert White's House and the Oates Museum, The Wakes, High Street, Selborne, Alton, Hampshire GU34 3JH.
  Telephone: 01420 511275. Website: www.gilbertwhiteshouse.org.uk Home of the Reverend Gilbert White (1720–93), the naturalist parson, forerunner of many Victorian clergymen scientists.

Wilberforce House, High Street, Hull, East Yorkshire HU1 1NQ.
  Telephone: 01482 300300. Website: www.hullcc.gov.uk A museum devoted to a leading Evangelical layman, William Wilberforce, the abolitionist.